Kill the Recipe: A Cookbook and Visual Guidebook on the Basics of Radical Beanmaking and Plant-based Eating

By Mark Andrew Gravel
Illustrated by Lucy Engelman

Published by foodsexart

ISBN-10: 0615599699
ISBN-13: 978-0615599694

"To the few who love me & whom I love -- to those who feel rather than those who think -- to the dreamers & those who put faith in dreams as in the only realities -- I offer this Book of Truths, not in its character of Truth-Teller, but for the Beauty that abounds in its Truth; constituting it true. To these I present the composition as an Art-Product alone: let us say as a Romance; or, if I be not urging too lofty a claim, as a poem."

- Edgar Allan Poe, *Eureka*

Plant-based Eating

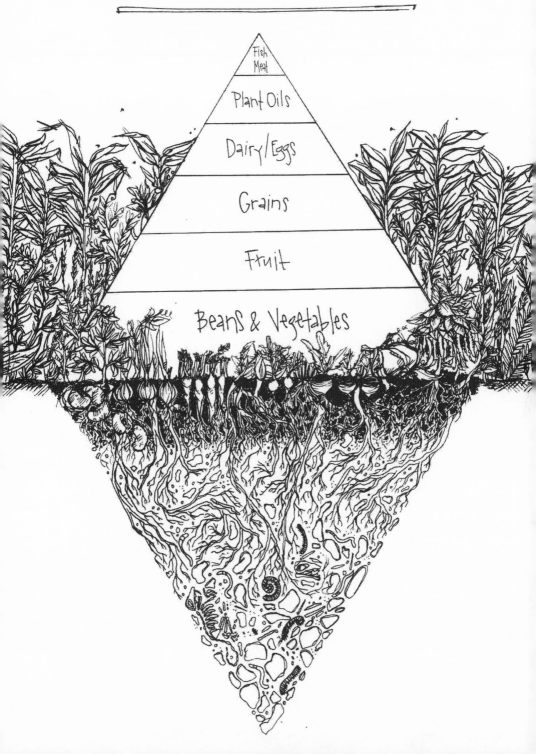

Beans for the Future

Kill the Recipe is a cookbook and visual guidebook on the basics of radical beanmaking and plant-based eating. Fundamentally, it is a vision for changing the way we think about cooking and eating in our homes. It proposes a new approach — one that is simple and straightforward, one that is affordable and lasting, and one that returns to tradition in order to imagine the future. As a part of this approach, it strives to contribute to the much-needed cultural shift in the way we eat and to truly advance our understanding of making good food at home in a way that will benefit our health and save both time and money. Kill the Recipe's fundamental focus is on beauty and usefulness. It is something you can bring into the kitchen and get dirty, something that compels you to cook in a way that brings value to your everyday life, and most of all, something that is accessible. I hope you find this book endlessly useful, and I hope it becomes a trusted journal full of your favorite ingredient combinations, clever cooking tricks, and food traditions both old and new. Ultimately, I hope it becomes a book you can pass on to future generations.

Beans for Food Security

Kill the Recipe reimagines our meals through the lens of beans. Practically, it illustrates how to create an endlessly variable number of healthy, convenient dishes from a simple pot of beans. Beans, after all, are a constant. They are among the oldest plant foods grown on earth and have sustained societies throughout history. They can also be found everywhere from farmers markets and bodegas to natural foods grocers and country stores. They make sense in any economic time and are an essential ingredient that brings great value, nutrition, and versatility to the kitchen. They set the stage to cook thrifty, satisfying meals with the rhythms of the season, and they allow you to smartly use what is at the market, on hand, or leftover. Furthermore, beans have an inherent capacity to improve our everyday quality of life as we work to better our food system. If we think of our food system as a recipe, with all its various parts functioning as ingredients, we can clearly see that our current recipe for feeding ourselves is not working that well. We need to think about how we can do things differently, starting in our own homes — the original spaces of economy — to make a better recipe for an affordable and lasting food system.

Basics

Beans are disarmingly easy to make - and by beans I'm broadly referring to all edible legumes. The following are basic guidelines that will help you use this book to its full potential.

Bean Cleaning
Sort through beans for pebbles and rinse well; rinse canned beans really well, too.

Vegetable Cleaning
Rinse and dry all vegetables, peel if necessary.

Aromatic Vegetables
Sweet and floral vegetables that are used to enhance flavor.

Salt, Fat, and Acid
Essential to any good pot of beans! Sea salt or kosher salt are best, animal fats and plant fats can be used interchangeably, and tart citrus can always be substituted for vinegar.

Equivalents
Dry beans expand to about three times their original size when cooked, so 1 cup of uncooked, dry beans equals 3 cups (+/-) of cooked beans.

Yield
When soaking dry beans for simmering, 2 cups will feed two people with leftovers; increase the amount of beans accordingly if you are cooking for more people. Similarly, one can of beans feeds two people.

Spices & Herbs

Kill the Recipe is designed as a framework for you to add your favorite flavor combinations in order to make the dishes your own. You can, in a sense, choose your own adventure. However, the following is a very basic spice and herb guide that will help you navigate the foundations of various cuisines.

Caribbean Cuisine
Curry, Nutmeg, Allspice, Clove, Coriander, Cinnamon, Oregano, Thyme

Chinese Cuisine
Star Anise, Clove, Cinnamon, Sichuan Peppercorn, White Pepper

French Cuisine
Green Peppercorn, Pink Peppercorn, Nutmeg, Tarragon, Thyme, Rosemary, Parsley, Marjoram, Chervil, Chive

German Cuisine
Caraway Seed, Juniper Berry, Allspice, White Pepper, Dry Mustard Powder, Cinnamon, Nutmeg, Paprika, Dill

Greek Cuisine
Cinnamon, Nutmeg, Oregano, Dill, Mint

Indian Cuisine
Aniseed, Cardamom Seed, Coriander Seed, Mustard Seed, Garam Masala, Fenugreek, Turmeric, Curry Powder, Clove, Cinnamon, Mace, Nutmeg, Saffron, Mint, Cilantro

Italian Cuisine
Fennel Seed, Basil, Parsley, Rosemary, Marjoram, Oregano

Mexican Cuisine
Cumin Seed, Coriander Seed, Annatto Seed, Cayenne, Achiote Powder, Oregano, Cilantro

Middle Eastern Cuisine
Aniseed, Caraway Seed, Cumin, Sumac, Baharat, Nutmeg, Cardamom, Turmeric, Allspice, Cinnamon

North African Cuisine
Cumin Seed, Coriander Seed, Turmeric, Paprika, Cinnamon, Saffron, Cilantro, Mint

Scandinavian Cuisine
Mustard Seed, Nutmeg, White Pepper, Cardamom, Dill

Spanish Cuisine
Cumin Seed, Parsley, Paprika, Saffron

Pantry Materials

You don't need many pantry materials to make good food because the best flavors are achieved by skillfully adding salt, fats, & acids to fresh ingredients. Tasting as you cook is the best way to learn.

carrot

dry beans

sea salt

garlic

other plant oils

SEA SALT

tomato paste

Sugar

raw or granulated sugar

red wine cider or white vinegar

dry grains
rice noodles couscous

spices of your choice

SALT

fennel

onion

kosher salt

Crushed red pepper

flour
all purpose
chickpea
rice
fine cornmeal

tomato sauce

extra virgin olive oil

black pepper

bay leaves

celery

Cooking Tools

You don't need too many cooking tools either, but here is a short list of basics that come in handy when needed. I recommend making food with your hands whenever possible.

blender

can opener

cutting board

measuring spoons

aluminum foil

salad spinner

measuring cups

cook's knife

ladle

vegetable peeler

serving spoon

whisk

wooden spoon

medium dutch oven

slotted spoon

spatula

medium mesh strainer

metal tongs

colander

immersion blender

whisk

medium frying pan

medium mixing bowl

kitchen towels

baking sheet

food processor

plastic wrap

medium stainless steel pot for boiling water

Notes

Weeknight Beans

When you don't have any cooked beans on hand to repurpose for a quick meal, weeknight beans offer a simple solution. Weeknight beans consist of boiling any can of beans you like in well-salted water with garlic, olive oil & crushed red pepper to significantly ———————— improve their flavor. ————————

When making, plan on one can of beans serving two people or one person with leftovers.

———————

To make weeknight beans, combine a can of drained, well-rinsed beans, ——————— a clove of garlic, a generous splash of olive oil, a few pinches of salt & a dash of crushed red pepper in a pot

add though water to just cover the beans, cover the pot with a lid, bring to a boil & continue cooking at a rolling boil for a 5 to 10 minutes

———————

When finished, drain & serve hot over cooked grains with a salad for a super quick meal or add them to any dish that calls for cooked beans

Notes

Soak

The goal of soaking dry beans is to rehydrate them. Soaking dry beans for 24 hours in well-salted water yields the best taste & texture & produces the shortest cooking time --30 to 90 minutes depending on the bean-- Split peas, lentils & canned beans do not need to be soaked

add beans & salt & cover with water by 3 inches

Let soak for 24 hrs. in well-salted water.

rinse well

[Large Pot]

drain

refrigerate for later

OR

Simmer

Notes

Simmer

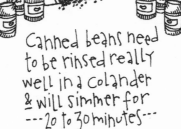

Dry beans that have been soaked & drained will simmer for ---30 to 90 minutes--- depending on the bean

Canned beans need to be rinsed really well in a colander & will simmer for ---20 to 30 minutes---

Dry Lentils & Split Peas do not need to be soaked & will simmer for --10 to 30 minutes--

add beans to the pot & cover with water by 1 inch

---- add ----

1/2 an onion

1 clove of garlic

a few bay leaves

a splash of olive oil

Bring the pot to a boil then reduce heat to low & simmer until tender

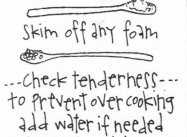

Skim off any foam

---Check tenderness--- to prevent over cooking add water if needed so beans do not dry out

when tender, turn off heat & a few small spoonfuls of salt

Serve hot over cooked grains with a salad or as a side dish or let them cool in their broth & refrigerate for later

MEALS FOREVER!

Notes

SOUP

Dice aromatic vegetables by hand or rough chop in a food processor

Carrot

Onion

Celery

Garlic

Fennel

Heat olive oil in a pot over medium heat. Add aromatic vegetables to the pot & season with salt & pepper

Let everything cook for 10 minutes while stirring occasionally

[Optional] Add a small amount of diced bacon, sausage or anchovy to cook with the aromatics

Once the aromatics are tender, add chopped leafy greens such as kale, collards, or spinach and/or any seasonal or leftover vegetables that are around

---Next---

add cooked, drained beans and enough liquid (beanbroth, stock or water) to cover the vegetables by 2-3 inches

[Optional]
Add any combination of spices that you like

Bring to a boil then reduce heat to medium-low & simmer uncovered for about 30 minutes until the flavors come together

Thin with more liquid if desired & adjust salt & pepper to taste

Serve with bread & a simple green salad

Notes

Stew

Dice aromatic vegetables by hand or rough chop in a food processor

fennel

garlic

carrot

onion

celery

Heat olive oil in a pot over medium heat

Add aromatic vegetables to the pot & season with salt & pepper

Let everything cook for about 10 minutes while stirring occasionally

[Optional] Add a small amount of diced bacon, sausage, or anchovy to cook with the aromatics

Once the aromatics are tender, add chopped leafy greens such as spinach, kale, or collards and/or any seasonal or leftover vegetables that are around

Next

add cooked, drained beans & enough liquid (bean broth, stock, or water) to cover the vegetables by 2-3 inches

STOCK   stock

Add any combination of spices that you like

30 MINUTES

Bring to a boil then reduce heat to medium-low & simmer uncovered for about 30 minutes until the flavors come together

Next, remove some of the mixture, puree it, & add it back to the pot or mash some of the beans by pressing them against the inside of the pot with a spoon or add a small amount of stale bread & continue simmering for an additional 15 to 30 minutes until the liquid thickens

OR

Thin with more liquid if it gets too thick & adjust salt and pepper to taste

Serve with potatoes, rice, or bread & a simple green salad

Notes

Casserole

Preheat oven to 350°F

Dice aromatic vegetables by hand or rough chop in a food processor

Heat olive oil in a pot over medium heat

Add aromatic vegetables to the pot & season with salt & pepper

Let everything cook for about 10 minutes while stirring occasionally

[Optional]
add sausage &/or bacon & brown until crispy on the outside

Add additional ingredients such as

tomato sauce   spices &/or chili paste   & a few splashes of water

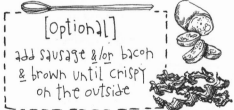

Cook for a few minutes to let the mixture come together

Add cooked, drained beans to the sauce, add a few drops of vinegar, & stir so the beans are evenly coated

In a small bowl, mix a couple handfuls of breadcrumbs with olive oil & a pinch of salt & stir until the mixture binds

Sprinkle the breadcrumb mixture over the beans

Bake uncovered at 350°F for about 10 minutes or until the dish is bubbling & the breadcrumbs are golden brown

Finish with fresh chopped herbs & serve immediately with a simple green salad

Notes

Sauced Beans

Dice aromatic vegetables by hand or rough chop in a food processor

Heat olive oil in a Pot over medium heat

Add aromatic vegetables to the Pot & season with salt & pepper

Let everything cook for about 10 minutes while stirring occasionally

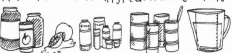

Add additional ingredients such as

tomato sauce, spices, &/or chili pastes & a generous splash of water to build the base of your sauce

Continue cooking for an additional 5 minutes while stirring occasionally

-----Next-----

add cooked, drained beans &

bean broth, stock, or water to the Pot, so the beans are just barely covered

Bring to a boil, then reduce heat to medium-low & simmer uncovered - - - for about 15 minutes - - - until the flavors come together

Thin with more liquid if the mixture gets too dry

Adjust salt & pepper to taste

Serve immediately over grains, as a side, or refrigerate for later use

Notes

Dressed Beans

Dice aromatic vegetables such as garlic & onion by hand

Warm olive oil in a frying pan over medium-high heat

Add aromatic vegetables to the frying pan & cook for one minute

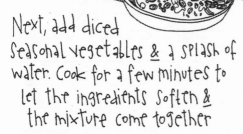

Next, add diced seasonal vegetables & a splash of water. Cook for a few minutes to let the ingredients soften & the mixture come together

[Spring] [Summer] [Fall] [Winter]

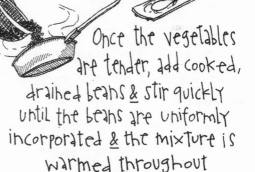

Once the vegetables are tender, add cooked, drained beans & stir quickly until the beans are uniformly incorporated & the mixture is warmed throughout

Adjust salt & pepper to taste

Add a few drops of vinegar, stir again, & serve with a little bit of meat, seafood, or eggs & a simple green salad

Notes

Salad

Dice or thinly slice aromatic &/or seasonal vegetables by hand

Add vegetables & cooked, drained beans to a mixing bowl

Add a drizzle of olive oil, a few splashes of vinegar, & season with salt & pepper

Mix gently to ensure that the beans & vegetables are spread evenly throughout the salad

Adjust salt & pepper to taste

Finish with chopped fresh herbs

Chives

parsley

Dill

Serve on its own with bread

or

with a little bit of meat, seafood, or eggs

Notes

Bean Purée

In a food processor, add

2 cups of cooked, drained beans

a small chopped onion

a couple cloves of chopped garlic

a few splashes of vinegar

a generous drizzle of olive oil, spices, & fresh herbs to taste & a few pinches of crushed red pepper

Season with salt & pepper

Pulse in the food processor until the ingredients come together into a smooth purée, scraping down the sides of the bowl with a spatula as needed

---

Add a few splashes of water if necessary to help the mixture come together, but keep the addition of water to to a minimum

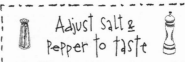

Adjust salt & pepper to taste

Transfer to a bowl & serve with vegetables & bread

or use as a sandwich spread

or refrigerate for later use

Notes

Fritters

In a food processor, add

2 cups of soaked,* drained beans

half of a small chopped onion

a couple cloves of chopped garlic

a splash of vinegar

Spices & fresh herbs to taste

a few pinches of crushed red pepper

salt & pepper

Pulse in the food processor until the ingredients come together into a coarse purée

If necessary, add a few small splashes of water to help the mixture come together, but keep the addition of water to a minimum so the fritters don't fall apart when you fry them

Adjust salt & pepper to taste

To cook the fritters, cover the bottom of a medium frying pan with 2 inches of vegetable oil

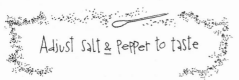

Heat the oil over medium heat until it is hot & shimmering but not smoking

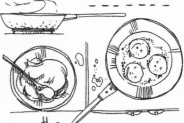

Once the oil is ready, scoop heaping tablespoons of the mixture into the pan & lightly press down the middle with the spoon to form small patties

Fry in batches, without crowding, until nicely browned, turning as necessary for about 3 to 5 minutes

Serve hot or at room temperature in a sandwich with lettuce & other thinly sliced raw vegetables or over a simple green salad with a tangy dressing

*use only soaked beans for these fritters, using cooked beans will cause them to fall apart

Notes

Bean Patty

In a food processor, add

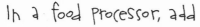

2 cups of cooked, drained beans

a couple cloves of chopped garlic

a splash of vinegar

(optional) a handful or two of a cooked seasonal or leftover vegetables

spices & fresh herbs to taste & a few pinches of crushed red pepper

Season with salt & pepper

Pulse in the food processor until the ingredients come together into a coarse purée, scraping down the sides of the bowl with a spatula as needed

If necessary, add a few drops of water to the mixture to help it come together, but keep the additional water to a minimum so the patties don't fall apart when you fry them

Adjust salt & pepper to taste

----- Next -----

transfer to a bowl & add one beaten egg & a handful of flour or breadcrumbs to bind the mixture

Continue adding the flour or breadcrumbs until the mixture thickens & you can easily form a patty

form the patties with your hands & dust the outside with a light coating of flour or breadcrumbs

To cook the patties, cover the bottom of a medium frying pan with a thin layer of vegetable oil

Heat the oil over medium heat until it is hot & shimmering but not smoking

Once the oil is ready, lightly press the patties into the pan & fry in batches, without crowding, until nicely browned, turning as necessary for about 5 minutes

Serve hot as a sandwich with lettuce & other thinly sliced raw vegetables or with a simple green salad

Notes

CRiSPY BeAHS

Preheat oven to 425°F

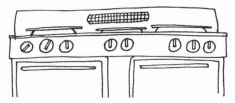

Place cooked, drained beans on a towel & gently pat dry

In a bowl, season the beans with olive oil, salt, pepper, & spices

--- Next ---

place beans on a well-oiled baking sheet & bake for approximately 25 minutes

Next, remove the baking sheet from the oven, rotate 180° & gently shake to make sure the beans are not sticking

Continue baking for 15 to 20 minutes or until the beans are crispy but not burnt

Once the beans are crispy, remove them from the oven, place in a mixing bowl, & finish with a drizzle of olive oil

Adjust salt & pepper to taste

Serve hot with fresh chopped herbs & a squeeze of lemon

Notes

Pancake

Preheat oven to 550°F

Let the batter rest for at least 10 minutes at room temperature

Once the batter is ready, cover the bottom of a medium frying pan or cast iron skillet with a thin layer of olive oil

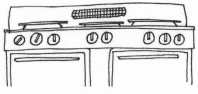

In a mixing bowl, add 2 cups of water for every 1½ cups of bean flour

whisk until the batter is smooth & slightly thick

Ladle the batter into the pan, place on the top shelf of the oven, & cook until the edges of the batter are set & the top is golden brown

- - - - - Next - - - - -

stir in a generous drizzle of olive oil, any combination of thinly sliced aromatic &/or seasonal vegetables & spices that you like

Season with salt & pepper

Transfer to a plate & finish with a drizzle of olive oil & salt, & serve with a simple green salad

Mark Andrew Gravel is an independent cook
and designer working at the intersection of
food and art. He is the founder of Good
Farm, an art and agriculture blog turned
foraging collective, and Bean-In, a yearlong
series of food happenings that culminated
with an all day temporary free restaurant at
California College of the Arts. Currently,
Mark runs Good Farm, freelances, and
continues to share his love for the culture
and diversity of beans through both
self-propelled and collaborative projects.

Lucy Engelman is an illustrator living in
Northfield, IL, where she plans her next
adventure. She attended the University of
Michigan in Ann Arbor, graduating with a
BFA in 2011. Her young career consists of
collaborations with chefs, farmers, artists,
designers of various trades, and publishers
from near and far. She has also received
recognition for her work in several
publications. Lucy is eager to continue
searching for inspiration in the fresh air
of the outdoors, pursuing an agrarian
inspired lifestyle, and collaborating with
professionals of all trades.

Glossary

Adzuki Bean
A small, dried, russet-colored bean with a sweet flavor, Adzuki beans can be purchased whole or powdered at Asian markets. They are particularly popular in Japanese cooking where they're used in confections such as the popular yokan, a jelly dessert made with adzuki bean paste, sugar, and agar.

Black Bean
Also called turtle beans, these dried beans have long been popular in Mexico, Central and South America, the Caribbean, and the southern United States. They have a black skin, cream-colored flesh and a sweet flavor, and form the base for the famous black-bean soup. They are commonly available in supermarkets.

Black-eyed Pea
This small beige bean has a black circular eye at its inner curve. It can also be called cowpea and, if the eye is yellow, yellow-eyed pea. Originating in Asia, the black-eyed pea is thought to have been introduced to the United States through the African slave trade. Though originally cultivated for animal fodder, black-eyed peas are now a popular legume (particularly in the South) and are essential in the traditional dish Hoppin' John. They can be purchased fresh or dried.

Cannellini Bean
Large, white Italian kidney beans, available both in dry and canned forms. Cannellini beans are particularly popular in salads and soups.

Chickpea
Slightly larger than the average pea, these round, irregular shaped, buff-colored legumes have a firm texture and mild, nutlike flavor. Chickpeas (also called garbanzo beans and ceci) are used extensively in the Mediterranean, India, and the Middle East for dishes such as couscous and hummus. They have also found their way into Spanish stews, Italian minestrone, and various Mexican dishes, and are quickly becoming popular in many parts of the Western and Southwestern United States. Chickpeas are available canned, dried, and, in some areas, fresh. They're most commonly used in salads, soups, and stews.

Cranberry Bean
Also called shell beans or shellouts, these beautiful beans have large, knobby beige pods splotched with red. The beans found inside are cream-colored with red streaks and have a delicious nutlike flavor. Cranberry beans must be shelled before cooking and lose their red color during the cooking process. They are available fresh in the summer and dried throughout the year.

Fava Bean

Also called faba bean, broad bean, or horse bean, this tan, rather flat bean resembles a very large lima bean. It comes in a large pod that, unless very young, is inedible. Fava beans can be purchased dried, cooked in cans, and occasionally fresh. If you find fresh fava beans, choose those with pods that are not bulging with beans, which indicates age. Fava beans have a very tough skin, which should be removed by blanching before cooking. They are very popular in Mediterranean and Middle Eastern dishes, can be cooked in a variety of ways, and are often used in soups.

Fermented Black Bean

Also called Chinese black beans and salty black beans, this Chinese specialty consists of small black soybeans that have been preserved in salt before being packed into cans or plastic bags. They have an extremely pungent, salty flavor and must be soaked in warm water for about 30 minutes before using. Fermented black beans are usually finely chopped before being added to fish or meat dishes as a flavoring. They can be stored tightly covered in a refrigerator for up to a year. If the beans begin to dry out, a few drops of peanut oil will refresh them.

Field Pea

A variety of yellow or green pea grown specifically for drying, these peas are dried and usually split along a natural seam, in which case they're called split peas. Whole and split dried field peas are available packaged in supermarkets and in bulk in health food stores. Field peas do not usually require presoaking before cooking.

Flageolet

These tiny, tender French kidney beans range in color from pale green to creamy white. They are rarely available fresh in the United States, but can be purchased dried, canned, and occasionally frozen. Flageolets are usually prepared simply in order to showcase their delicate flavor. They're a classic accompaniment to lamb and also a popular choice for the French country dish, cassoulet.

Fresh Bean

Fresh beans are those that are commercially available in their fresh form and are generally sold in their pods. The three most commonly available fresh-bean varieties are green beans, which are eaten with their shell or pod, and lima and fava beans, both of which are eaten shelled. Store fresh beans in a tightly covered container in the refrigerator up to 5 days; after that amount of time, both color and flavor begin to diminish. If cooked properly, fresh beans contain a fair amount of vitamins A and C; lima beans are also a good source of protein.

Great Northern Bean

These beans are large white beans that resemble lima beans in shape but that have a delicate, distinctive flavor. They're grown in the Midwest and are generally available dried. As with other dried beans, they must be soaked before cooking. Great Northern beans are particularly popular in baked bean dishes and can be substituted for any white beans in most recipes.

Green Bean

The green bean has a long, slender green pod with small seeds inside. The entire pod is edible. It's also called string bean (because of the fibrous string — now bred out of the species — that used to run down the pod's seam) and snap bean (for the sound the bean makes when broken in half.) The wax bean is a pale yellow variety of green bean. Green beans are available year-round, with a peak season of May to October. Choose slender beans that are crisp, bright-colored and free of blemishes. Store in the refrigerator, tightly wrapped in a plastic bag, for up to 5 days. Cook gently by steaming or simmering just until tender and crisp. Green beans have a fair amount of vitamins A and C.

Kidney Bean

Particularly popular for chili con carne and red beans and rice, this firm, medium-size bean has a dark red skin and cream-colored flesh. Its popularity can be attributed to its full-bodied flavor. Unless you live in an area that grows kidney beans, it is difficult find them fresh and you will have to settle for the dried or canned forms. White kidney beans — referred to as cannellini beans — lack the robust flavor of their red cousins, and are only available dried or canned. The tiny, tender French kidney beans are called flageolets and may be purchased dried, canned, and occasionally frozen.

Lima Bean

Although occasionally referred to as the Madagascar bean, this New World bean was named for Lima, Peru, where it was found as early as 1500. There are two distinct varieties of lima — the Fordhook and the baby lima. Both are pale green, plump-bodied, and have a slight kidney-shape curve. The Fordhook is larger and plumper than the baby lima. It also has a fuller flavor than its smaller relative. Fresh limas are available from June to September. They are usually sold in their pods, which should be plump, firm, and dark green. The pods can be refrigerated in a plastic bag for up to a week. They should be shelled just before using. Frozen lima beans are available year-round and are labeled according to variety (Fordhook or baby.) Canned and dried limas are usually labeled jumbo, large, or small, a designation that relates to size and not variety. In the South, dried limas are frequently referred to as butter beans. When mottled with purple they are designated as calico or speckled butter beans. A traditional way to serve these beans is with corn in succotash. They are also used alone as a side dish, in soups and sometimes in salads. Lima beans contain a good amount of protein, phosphorus, potassium, and iron.

Lentil

Popular in parts of Europe and a staple throughout much of the Middle East and India, this tiny, lens-shaped pulse has long been used as a meat substitute. There are three main varieties of lentils. The French or European lentil, sold with the seed coat on, has a grayish-brown exterior and a creamy yellow interior. The reddish orange Egyptian or red lentil is smaller, rounder and sans seed coat. There is also a yellow lentil. None of these varieties are used fresh, but are instead dried as soon as they become ripe. The regular brown lentils are commonly found in supermarkets, whereas the red and yellow lentils, though available in some supermarkets, usually must be purchased in Middle Eastern or East Indian markets. Lentils should be stored airtight at room temperature and will keep up to a year. They can be used as a side dish (pureed, whole and combined with vegetables), in salads, soups, and stews. One of the most notable showcases for the lentil is the spicy East Indian dal. Lentils have a fair amount of calcium and vitamins A and B, and are a good source of iron and phosphorus.

Marrow Bean

Grown chiefly in the East, these are the largest and roundest of the white beans. Typically found fresh only in the region where they are grown, these beans are available dried year-round in most supermarkets. Marrow beans are customarily served sauced as a side dish in the manner of pasta.

Mung Bean

These are small dried beans with yellow flesh and a skin that is normally green but sometimes yellow or black. These beans are most commonly used to grow bean sprouts. Mung beans are widely used in both China and India. They need no presoaking and, when cooked, they have a tender texture and slightly sweet flavor. Dried mung beans are ground into flour, which is used to make noodles in China and a variety of dishes in India.

Navy Bean

This small white legume, also known as Yankee bean, gets its name from the fact that the U.S. Navy has served it as a staple since the mid 1800s. The navy bean is widely used for commercially canned pork and beans. It also makes wonderful soups and is often used in the preparation of Boston baked beans (though New Englanders prefer using the smaller pea bean for this purpose.) Navy beans require lengthy, slow cooking.

Pea Bean

The smallest of the dried white beans, the others being navy, great northern, and marrow beans (in order of ascending size.) Pea beans are very popular in the Northeast and are the first choice for Boston baked beans. Some producers and packagers do not differentiate between pea beans and navy beans, so packages identified as white beans may contain both. Pea beans are also used in soups. They require long, slow cooking.

Pink Bean

This is a smooth, reddish-brown dried bean that is very popular in the western United States. This bean is interchangeable with the pinto bean in most dishes. Pink beans are used to make refried beans and chili con carne. They are available in dried form in most supermarkets.

Pinto Bean

The pinto (Spanish for painted) bean has streaks of reddish-brown on a background of pale pink. The beans are grown in the United States Southwest and are common in most Spanish-speaking countries, where they are often served with rice or used in soups and stews. The pinto can be used interchangeably with the pink bean, which is lighter in color prior to cooking but looks the same afterwards. Both the pinto and pink bean are commonly used in the preparation of refried beans and chili con carne. Pinto beans are available in dried form year-round. They are also called red Mexican beans.

Red Bean

Popular in Mexico and the southwestern United States, this dark red, medium-size bean is a favorite for making chili con carne (with beans) and refried beans (refritos.) Red beans are also popular in Louisiana's red beans and rice. Red beans are available dried in most supermarkets.

Runner Bean

This climbing plant — one of Britain's favorite green beans — was brought to the British Isles in the 17th century for decorative use because of its beautiful flowers. The scarlet runner bean has a long, green bean type pod that holds red streaked beige, medium-size seeds. Young runners may be prepared in any way suitable for green beans. In U.S. markets, consumers are more likely to find the shelled dried beans, which can be cooked like pinto or pink beans and used in dishes such as soups and stews.

Soybean

It's thought that the first written record of soybeans is dated 2838 B.C., and the Chinese have been cultivating them for thousands of years. So important are soybeans to the Chinese that they are considered one of the five sacred grains along with rice, wheat, barley and millet. Soybeans did not find their way to Japan until the 6th century and to Europe until the 17th century. Their extraordinary nutritive value was not scientifically confirmed until the 20th century. Although the United States failed to show significant interest in soybeans until the 1920s, it now supplies one-third of the world's total production. There are over 1,000 varieties of this nutritious legume, ranging in size from as small as a pea to as large as a cherry. Soybean pods, which are covered with a fine tawny to gray fuzz, range in color from tan to black. The beans themselves come in various combinations of red, yellow, green, brown and black. Their flavor is generally quite bland, which may explain why they were not embraced by Western cultures until their nutritive value was discovered. Unlike other legumes, the soybean is low in carbohydrates and high in protein and desirable oil. Because they are inexpensive and nutrition-packed, soybeans are used to produce a wide variety of products including tofu (soybean curd), soybean oil, soy flour, soymilk, soy sauce, miso, and tamari. Soybeans can be cooked (after being presoaked) like any other dried bean to be used in soups, stews, casseroles, etc. They can also be sprouted and used in salads or as a cooked vegetable. Additionally, soybean by-products are used in making margarines, as emulsifiers in many processed foods, and in nonfood items such as soaps and plastics. Fresh soybeans are not generally available except in Asian markets or specialty produce markets in late summer and early fall. Dried soybeans, beans for sprouting, and a huge variety of soybean products are available in supermarkets and health food stores. The soybean is also called soya bean, soy pea, soja and soi.

Sprouts

These include the crisp, tender sprouts of various germinated beans and seeds. Mung bean sprouts, used often in Chinese cooking, are the most popular. However, other seeds and beans — such as alfalfa and radish seeds, lentils, soybeans and wheat berries — may also be sprouted. For optimum crispness, sprouts are best eaten raw. They may also be stir-fried or sautéed, but should only be cooked for 30 seconds or less; longer cooking will wilt the sprouts. Though you may grow your own fresh sprouts, they are also available in most large supermarkets. Choose crisp looking sprouts with the buds attached; avoid musty-smelling, dark or slimy looking sprouts. Mung bean sprouts should be refrigerated in a plastic bag for no more than 3 days. More delicate sprouts — like alfalfa sprouts — should be refrigerated in the ventilated plastic container in which they are usually sold and kept for no more than 2 days. Canned mung bean sprouts — available in most supermarkets — fundamentally lack the texture or flavor of fresh.

Winged Bean

Also called goa bean, this tropical legume is rapidly becoming a
staple throughout the poorer regions of the world where it grows.
The reasons are basic: it grows quickly, is disease resistant, and
is high in protein. The winged bean is also valued because it is
entirely edible, including the shoots, flowers, roots, leaves, pods
and seeds. The pods, which can be green, purple or various shades
of red, are four-sided and flare from the center into ruffled
ridges or wings. These beans have a flavor similar to that of a
cranberry bean with a hint of green bean. The texture is like that
of a starchy green bean. Winged beans may be found in specialty
produce markets and some supermarkets. Choose small beans with no
sign of discoloration. Refrigerate, tightly wrapped in a plastic
bag, for up to 3 days. Wash and trim these beans before using.
Winged beans may be prepared in any way suitable for green beans.

Yard-long Bean

Yard-long beans are pencil-thin legumes that resemble a green bean
but can grow up to about 3 feet long (though it's usually picked at
18 inches or less.) Yard-long beans belong to the same plant family
as the black-eyed pea. In fact, in parts of China, the bean is
allowed to mature until full-fledged peas are produced in the pod.
Yard-longs have a flavor similar to but not as sweet as that of a
green bean, with hints of its black-eyed pea lineage. The texture
of the pod is more pliable and not as crisp as that of a green
bean. This legume, also called Chinese long bean, long bean, or
asparagus bean, can be found year-round (with peak season in the
fall) in most Asian markets and some supermarkets with specialty
produce sections. Select those that are small (which equates to
younger) and very flexible; the peas should not have matured.
Refrigerate in a plastic bag for up to 5 days. Yard-long beans are
most often cut into 2 inch lengths and sautéed or stir-fried.
Overcooking will make them mushy. These beans are rich in vitamin A
and contain a fair amount of vitamin C.

Via Epicurious (© Copyright Barron's Educational Services, Inc.
1995 based on *The Food Lover's Companion*, 2nd edition, by Sharon
Tyler Herbst)

Beans are Culture
Lila Bola Roja
Kashmiri Rajma
Laird Pinto
Pink
Green Split
Vaquero
Ayocote Morado
Val
Steuben
Butterscotch
Tongues of Fire
Bolita
Small Red
Red Spanish
Eston Green
Pardina
Flageolet
Mayacoba
Rebosero
Tepary
Pebbles
Petite Crimson
Cannellini
Rice
Corona
Alubia
Jackson Wonder
Chickpea
Baby Lima
Black Calypso
Bird Egg
Navy
Christmas Lima
Rio Zape
Ojo de Cabra
Yellow Indian Woman
Good Mother
Santa Maria
Runner Cannelli
Pinquito
Vallarta
Black Valentine
Garbanzo
Cranberry
Arikara
Anasazi
Molasses Face
Canary

16802516R10033

Made in the USA
Charleston, SC
11 January 2013